Dinosaurs

on the
MAP

Alix Wood

PowerKiDS
press

New York

Published in 2015 by Rosen Publishing
29 East 21st Street, New York, NY 10010

Copyright © 2015 by the Rosen Publishing Group, Inc.
Produced for Rosen by Alix Wood Books

Editor for Alix Wood Books: Eloise Macgregor
Designer: Alix Wood
US Editor: Joshua Shadowens
Researcher: Kevin Wood
Geography Consultant: Kerry Shepheard, B.Ed (Hons) Geography

Photo credits: All images © Shutterstock, except; 7 bottom © National Museum
and Research Center of Altamira; 21 © USGS; 23 bottom and middle © Alix Wood;
24 bottom left © Michael Rissi

Publisher's Cataloging Data

Wood, Alix.
Dinosaurs on the map / by Alix Wood.
p. cm. — (Fun with map skills)
Includes index.
ISBN 978-1-4777-6960-7 (library binding) — ISBN 978-1-4777-6961-4 (pbk.) —
ISBN 978-1-4777-6962-1 (6-pack)
1. Dinosaurs—Juvenile literature. 2. Navigation—History—Juvenile literature.
3. Maps—Juvenile literature. I. Wood, Alix. II. Title.
QE862.D5 W69 2015
910.4—d23

Manufactured in the United States of America

CPSIA Compliance Information: Batch #WS14PK9: For Further Information contact Rosen Publishing, New York, New York at 1-800-237-9932

3 7777 12913 7915

Contents

Mapping the Earth

A map is a diagram of the Earth's surface, or part of it. Maps can be of a large area, like a **continent**, or they can be of a very small area, like your bedroom! Maps record where things are in the world. It would be very difficult to show someone where something was without a map. Maps let you know what to expect when you go to a place. They also help you know if you are going in the right direction.

No one type of map can show you everything. We need lots of different kinds of maps. A map that can show you where to look for dinosaur **fossils** will look very different from a map that shows you where to look for a restaurant. A globe is shaped like a ball, which is almost the same shape as the Earth itself. Because it is the same shape, a globe can show you how the Earth really looks. It can't show you much detail, though.

a globe

an image of the Earth taken from a satellite

Do You Know?

The land on Earth is constantly changing shape. The changes are usually very small, but sometimes a new island can appear!

Maps are usually flat. People who make maps have to turn the curved Earth's surface into a flat drawing. These types of maps are called **projections**. They change the shape of the continents a little.

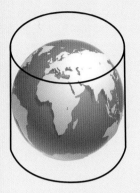

▶ This map is made using the Mercator projection. It is drawn as though a sheet of paper had been wrapped around the globe. The areas around the middle are accurate, but the areas to the top and bottom of the map are distorted.

When Dinosaurs Walked on Earth

Back when dinosaurs were alive, the Earth looked very different! There was one huge continent, and one vast ocean. We know this because people have found fossils of similar or identical species in countries that are now great distances apart. We call the continent Pangaea, and the ocean Panthalassa.

▲ How the Earth looked 200 million years ago!

▲ How the Earth looks now.

Symbols and Keys

If you were looking for a dinosaur museum on a map, what should you look for? Maps often use pictures instead of words to show where things are. These pictures are called symbols. Symbols can be of natural features such as rivers, or man-made features such as dinosaur museums. Symbols need to be clear and simple. Three trees could be a symbol for a forest, or a "P" could be a symbol for a parking lot. A map key or legend says what the map symbols stand for.

Below is a map of Dinosaur, Colorado. The town is called Dinosaur because it is near Dinosaur National Monument, where many dinosaur fossils have been found. Several roads are named after dinosaurs!

Try Your Skills

Can you work out which symbol is which?
1. Café
2. Hotel
3. Post Office
4. Point of Interest
5. Parking

a) **P**

b) ★

c) ✉

d) ☕

e) 🛏

Key

	Main Street
	Residential Street
	Under Construction
	Building
	Park

Follow the Caveman's Hunting Map

Early man, called hominids, did not exist when dinosaurs walked on Earth. Dinosaurs became **extinct** 65 million years ago! The earliest known cave drawing is around 40,000 years old. Hominids were around at the same time as saber-toothed tigers and woolly mammoths though! Before people learned to write, early man would draw directions by marking on the walls or the sandy floor of their cave.

Imagine you have stumbled across this hunting map in a cave. Can you work out which path to take to hunt which animal?

1. Bison
2. Woolly mammoth
3. Saber-toothed tiger

Which path has to cross the lake?

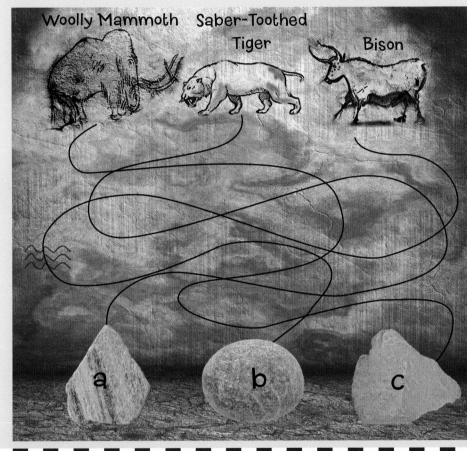

Key

lake

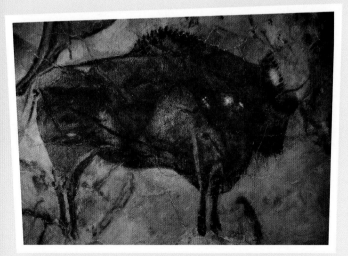

▲ This cave painting of a bison from Altamira, Spain is around 15,000 years old!

Do You Know?

The earliest hominids who used stone tools were *Homo habilis*. They lived around 2.3 million years ago.

Dinosaur Hunt

When you are looking for something on a map, it is much easier to find if you know where to start looking. A grid helps with map reading as it divides the map into squares. You can tell someone exactly what square an object is in to help them find it. Some dinosaurs are wandering around in the map below. See if you can find them using the **grid references**.

◀ This dinosaur is a compsognathus. It was about the same size as a turkey!

Find the first number along the x **axis**. Then find the number that goes up the y axis. You can remember the order by saying "Go along the corridor and then up the stairs."

Do You Know?

The number always refers to the bottom left hand corner of the square.

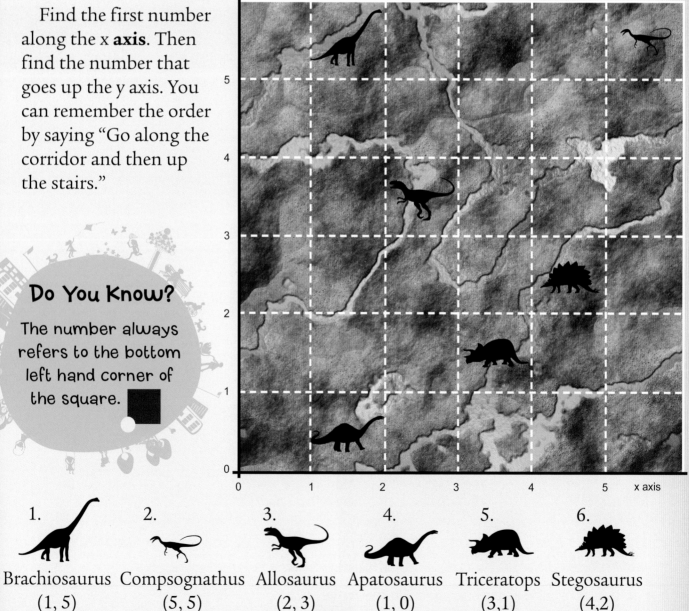

1. Brachiosaurus (1, 5)

2. Compsognathus (5, 5)

3. Allosaurus (2, 3)

4. Apatosaurus (1, 0)

5. Triceratops (3,1)

6. Stegosaurus (4,2)

8

Hide! *Tyrannosaurus rex* Is Hungry!

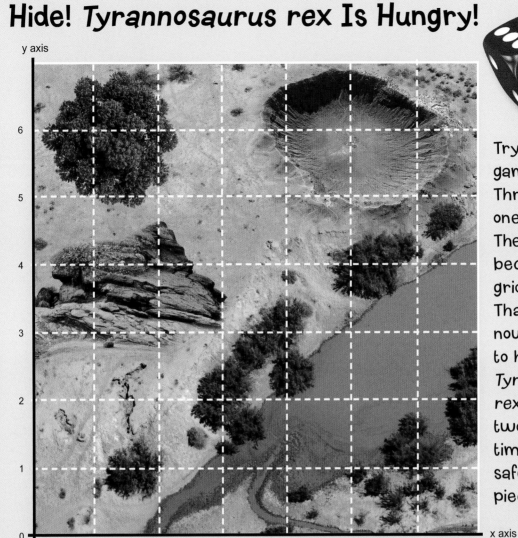

y axis

6

5

4

3

2

1

0

0   1   2   3   4   5   6   x axis

Try playing this game with a friend. Throw two dice, one at a time. The numbers become your grid reference. That square is now a safe place to hide from the *Tyrannosaurus rex*. Throw the two dice six more times. Mark each safe square with a piece of paper.

Then take turns to throw the dice ten times each. See how many times you land on a safe square, and how many times you get eaten by T. rex! The one that is eaten the most loses! Remember-the first number is the x axis, the second number is the y axis.

▶ *Tyrannosaurus rex* lived in western North America. "Tyrannosaurus" means "tyrant lizard" and "rex" means "king."

9

Fossil Hunt

We know about dinosaurs from studying their fossils. A fossil is the **prehistoric** remains of a plant or animal. Fossils are formed when the plant or dead animal is buried under layers of sand and mud. Under great pressure the sand and mud become rock. Minerals seep into the fossil, and create a replica in stone!

▲ A fossilized lizard

A fossil can be a trace or a body fossil. Body fossils form from the body or bodypart of a creature or plant. Trace fossils are fossilized signs of plant and animal activity, for example, dinosaur tracks, trails, and dung are all trace fossils.

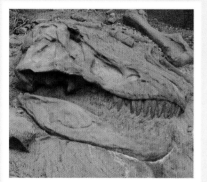

▲ A body fossil

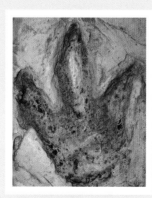

▲ A trace fossil

Do You Know?

To be called a fossil, scientists have decided the remains have to be over 10,000 years old!

The Earth's crust floats on the hot melted rock that makes up the Earth's mantle. The crust is made up of several large sections called plates which gradually shift around. Events such as a volcano erupting, or the plates colliding at speed can lead to rock that was buried deep underground being pushed to the surface. This rock will sometimes contain fossils.

▶ These layers of rock have been pushed up sideways! The older layers on the right would have been deep underground.

Look at this picture of a beach and some cliffs. If you were hunting for dinosaur fossils, where would you be most likely to find some?

a) In the sea
b) On the beach
c) In the woods
d) In the cliffs

the woods

the cliffs

the sea

the beach

Make Your Own "Hide a Fossil" Game

You will need some soil or sand, some sticks, and a seed tray or roasting dish. Fill the tray with the soil or sand. Place the sticks over the tray to make a grid. Write labels for the grid and stick them in the sand. Now bury a "fossil" in the soil. You can use a stone or a small plastic toy. Write the coordinates on a piece of paper for your fossil-hunting friend to use to find the fossil.

3

2

1

0   1   2

Finding Your Way

Maps are used to show routes of how to get from one place to another. Sometimes the maps don't look much like the place they are describing. These maps concentrate on showing how to move from one road or track to another, so that you can find your way. Road maps and public transport maps are good examples of this kind of route planner.

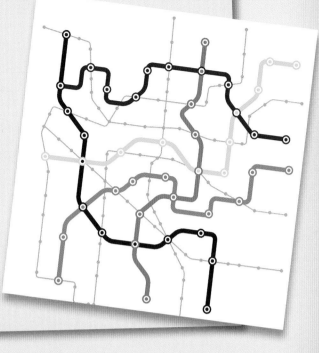

The Lost Eggs

Can you follow directions? This little ceratosaurus has lost her eggs. Use the key to follow these directions and help her find them.

Go along the sandy path until you meet the river. Turn right and head upriver. Take the first track on the right through the trees. Cross the river. The eggs are under the first tree.

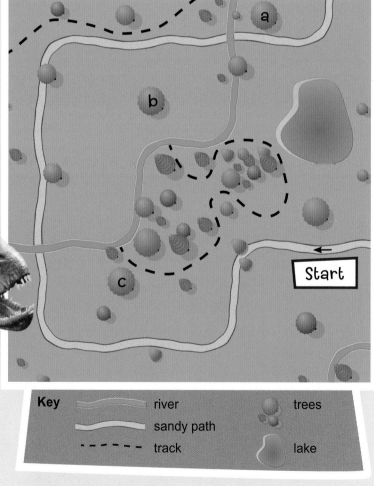

Key
river   trees
sandy path
- - - track   lake

Are the eggs under
1. tree a?   2. tree b?   3. tree c?

A map can show how far a journey is. Most maps will have a **scale** on them. As maps are not the same size as the places they show, the scale uses one unit of measurement, for example an inch (cm) to represent another unit of measurement, such as a mile (km). This scale shows 1 inch = 1 mile, 1.58 cm = 1 km.

0	1	2	3 miles
0	1	2	3	4	5 km

Try Your Skills

You can use the scale to measure distances. Use a piece of string to measure the trails taken by these dinosaurs. Then measure the string along the scale and work out how far they traveled.

1. Which dinosaur walked the longest distance?
2. Which dinosaur traveled the shortest distance?

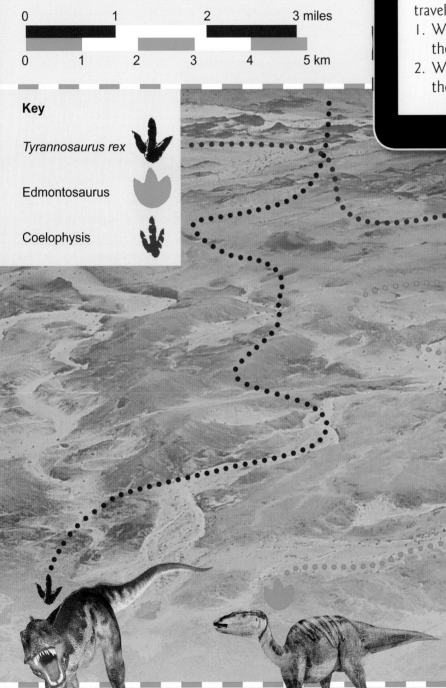

Key

Tyrannosaurus rex

Edmontosaurus

Coelophysis

Drawing Dinosaurs to Scale

As dinosaurs are extinct it is hard to imagine how big different types of dinosaurs were. Some museums have life-size skeletons or models. If you are not lucky enough to live near such a museum, you need to find a picture of the dinosaur drawn to scale. The dinosaur is drawn next to another animal that we know the size of. For large dinosaurs, scale drawings usually compare the dinosaur with a human. Smaller dinosaurs might be compared with a cat or a rat.

Scale

Camarasaurus Giganotosaurus Torosaurus Dilophosaurus

Ornitholestes

Compsognathus

How Much Bigger?

A scale can be written as a **ratio**. The scale 1:100 means that one unit of measurement on a map is the same as 100 units of measurement in real life. This means that 1 cm on a map represents 1 meter in the real world, or 1 inch on the map represents 100 inches.
Measure the man on the right from head to toe in centimeters. An average height man is 1.8 meters tall.

1. How may times bigger than the drawing is a man in real life?
2. What is the ratio?
3. How tall was this Aucasaurus?

Do You Know?

Some dinosaurs were tiny. A newly discovered dinosaur called a Microraptor was around the same size as a crow!

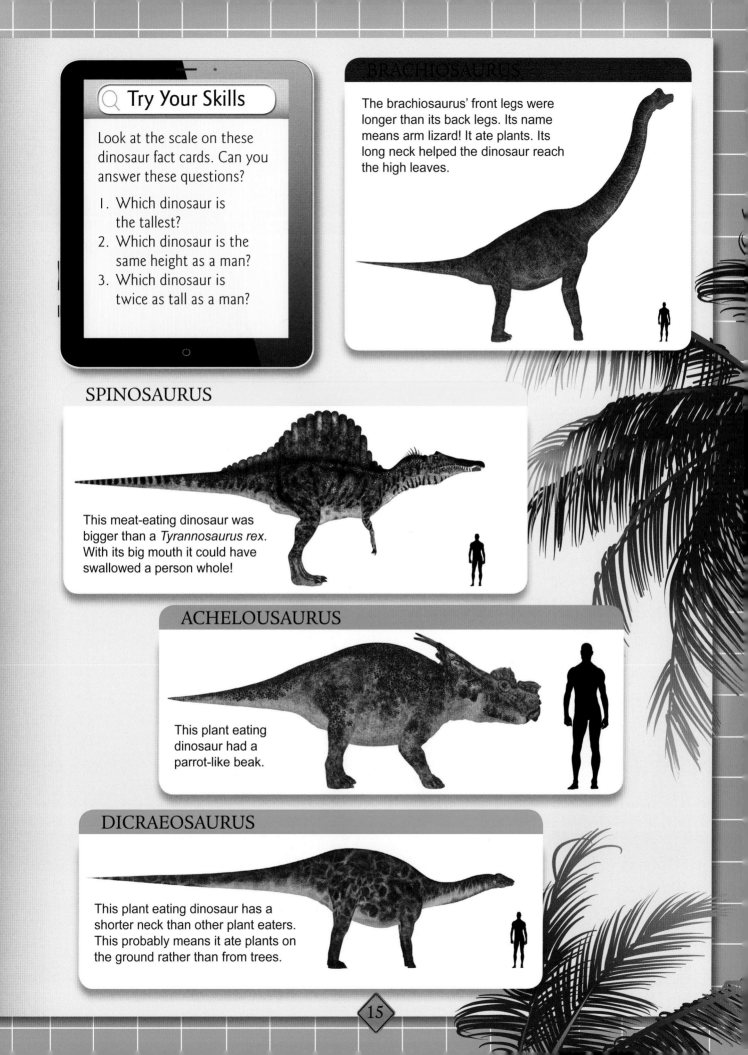

Try Your Skills

Look at the scale on these dinosaur fact cards. Can you answer these questions?

1. Which dinosaur is the tallest?
2. Which dinosaur is the same height as a man?
3. Which dinosaur is twice as tall as a man?

BRACHIOSAURUS

The brachiosaurus' front legs were longer than its back legs. Its name means arm lizard! It ate plants. Its long neck helped the dinosaur reach the high leaves.

SPINOSAURUS

This meat-eating dinosaur was bigger than a *Tyrannosaurus rex*. With its big mouth it could have swallowed a person whole!

ACHELOUSAURUS

This plant eating dinosaur had a parrot-like beak.

DICRAEOSAURUS

This plant eating dinosaur has a shorter neck than other plant eaters. This probably means it ate plants on the ground rather than from trees.

15

Using a Compass

The Earth is like a giant magnet. The north and south poles are magnetic. A compass has a magnetic needle which will always point to the **north magnetic pole**. The **compass rose** shows the points of the compass. The four main **cardinal directions** are north, south, east, and west.

Maps will usually have a drawing of a compass rose on them. On most maps north points toward the top of the map. If you go clockwise around the compass the main points are north, then east, then south, and finally west. They are usually written using just their first letter, N, E, S, and W.

Do You Know?

An easy way to remember the points of the compass is to say this phrase: **Never Eat Slimy Worms.**

Cardinal Directions

This nedoceratops needs some help. Use the compass above to help you show him which way to go

1. to the lake
2. to his friend
3. to the mountains
4. to the woods

a) **W**
b) **S**
c) **N**
d) **E**

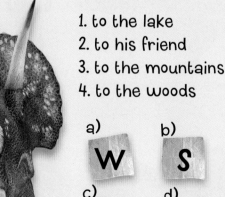

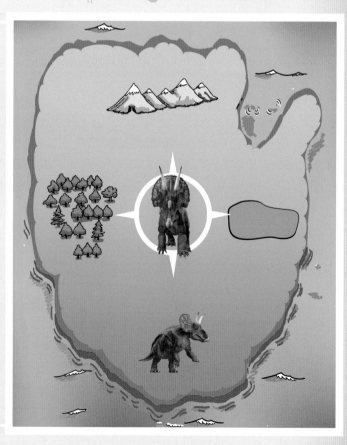

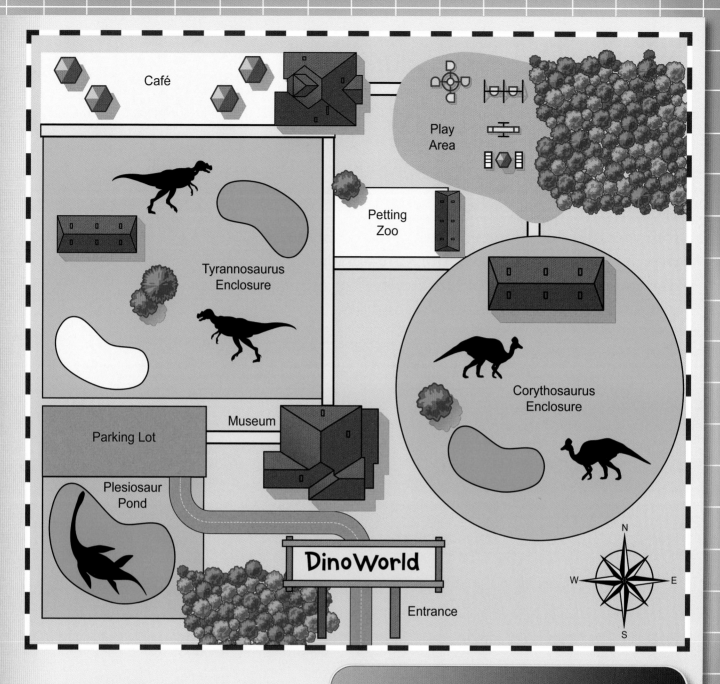

Café

Play Area

Petting Zoo

Tyrannosaurus Enclosure

Corythosaurus Enclosure

Parking Lot

Museum

Plesiosaur Pond

DinoWorld

Entrance

N
W   E
S

Above is a map of a dinosaur theme park. The map tells you how to get from place to place. The map has a compass rose to tell you what direction you need to go to get to the different attractions. Use the map to explore the park and to help you answer the questions on the right.

🔍 Try Your Skills

Can you answer these questions?
1. What direction should you walk to get from the parking lot to the museum?
2. Is the corythosaurus enclosure to the north or the south of the play area?
3. What direction should you walk to get from the parking lot to the plesiosaurs?
4. What direction should you walk from the petting zoo to the tyrannosaurus' pond?

17

Where Did Dinosaurs Live?

Dinosaur remains have been found all around the world. See if you can find your favorite dinosaurs on the map below. To answer the questions, you'll need to learn some more compass directions. **Intermediate directions** are halfway between the four cardinal directions of north, south, east, and west. The intermediate directions are northeast, northwest, southeast, and southwest. They are usually shortened to NE, NW, SE, and SW.

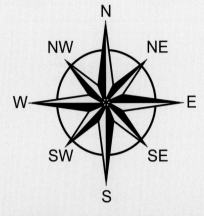

Pterodactyl

Lambeosaurus

Spinosaurus

Titanosaurus

Massospondylus

Argentinosaurus

🔍 Try Your Skills

Imagine you are a fossil hunter. What direction would you need to travel to find the next dinosaur?

1. Argentinosaurus to spinosaurus?
2. Titanosaurus to lambeosaurus?
3. Pterodactyl to spinosaurus?
4. Spinosaurus to titanosaurus?

Dinosaur Habitats

A habitat is the type of environment an animal lives in. Different dinosaurs lived in different habitats. Can you tell where each of the dinosaurs below would live on this habitat map? Use the clues in the pictures to help you.

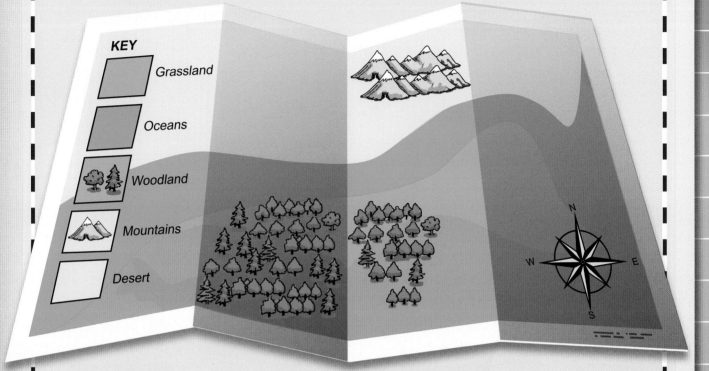

KEY

Grassland

Oceans

Woodland

Mountains

Desert

1. Coelophysis

2. Plesiosaur

3. Triceratops

4. Dicraeosaurus

Where Are the Best Fossils?

Plant and animal remains were most often fossilized if they were buried quickly. **Floodplains**, lakes, ponds, and river **deltas** were good areas for forming fossils. Small pieces of crumbling rocks, called **sediment**, would collect there. Sediment helps make the fossil. Sediment can be found in areas of the seabed too, so ocean dinosaurs were fossilized, too.

Before looking for fossils, dinosaur experts look at **geologic** maps. These maps show where sedimentary rock can be found at the surface of the earth. If they are looking for land dinosaur fossils, they will search for sedimentary rock that formed on land. Fossil hunters don't just look in any sedimentary rock though. The rock needs to be the right age. Dinosaur fossils can only be found in rock that formed during the Mesozoic era. Geologic history is divided into periods of years called eras. The Mesozoic era was between 252 and 65.6 million years ago!

Do You Know?

The Mesozoic era was made up of three periods. The Triassic, Jurassic, and Cretaceous periods.

◀ This young triceratops lived in the late Cretaceous period. Dinosaurs thrived in this period, until they suddenly became extinct. This may have been due to an asteroid colliding with the Earth.

Dinosaur Hunts and Geologic Maps

Geologic maps show different ages of rock in an area. The map below was produced by the United States Geological Survey. This map color-codes the rock, so you can see at a glance the best areas for finding different types of dinosaur fossils.

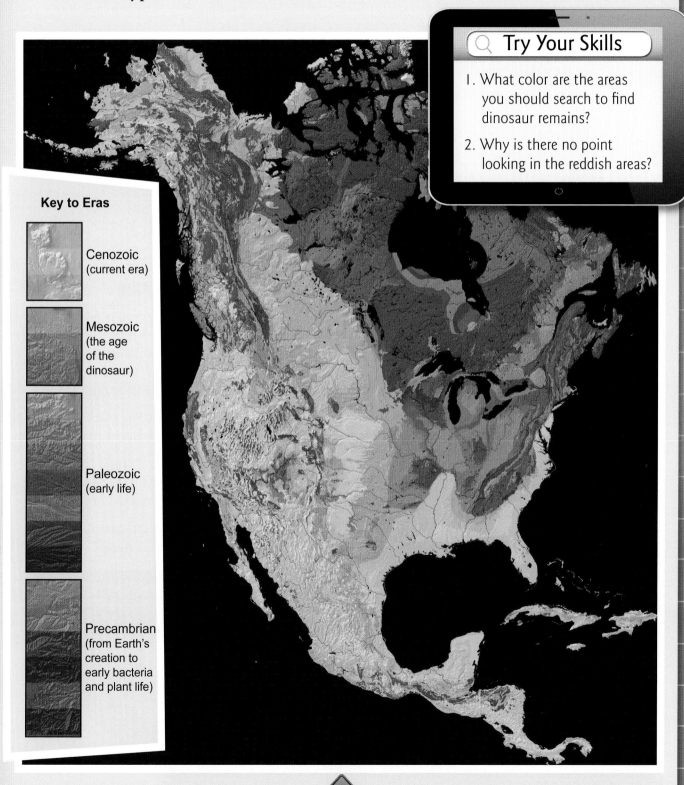

Key to Eras

Cenozoic (current era)

Mesozoic (the age of the dinosaur)

Paleozoic (early life)

Precambrian (from Earth's creation to early bacteria and plant life)

Try Your Skills

1. What color are the areas you should search to find dinosaur remains?

2. Why is there no point looking in the reddish areas?

Rock Strata

Geologic maps may show the types of rock, as well as the age of the rock. Rock usually forms in layers, like in this photo of a cliff face. These layers are usually flat. Sometimes the layers will tilt like in the photo on page 10. A later event, such as a volcano erupting, will have forced the rock upward.

There are three different types of rock; sedimentary, metamorphic, and igneous. How are different types of rock formed? Heat produces changes. When you put cookie dough in an oven, the heat changes the dough and makes a cookie. A similar thing happens to rocks under the Earth's surface. As the Earth's crust moves, rocks can get pulled down to where temperatures are hot enough to melt them! Rocks can also change without completely melting, too. Pressure from the weight of the rocks above combined with the heat leads to a metamorphosis. Metamorphosis means change.

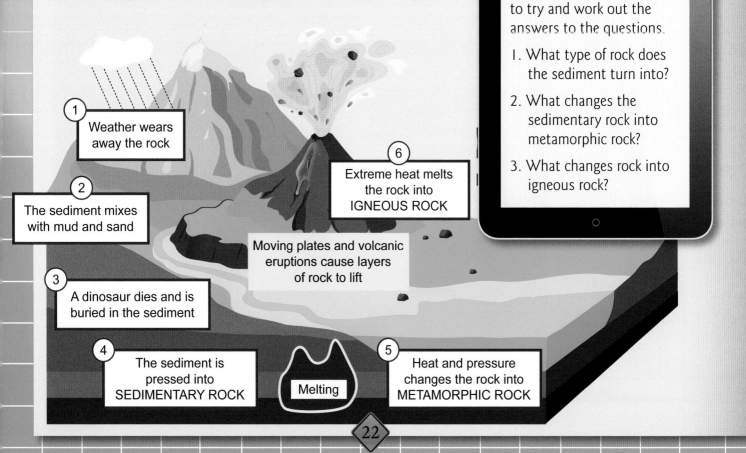

1 Weather wears away the rock

2 The sediment mixes with mud and sand

3 A dinosaur dies and is buried in the sediment

4 The sediment is pressed into SEDIMENTARY ROCK

Melting

5 Heat and pressure changes the rock into METAMORPHIC ROCK

6 Extreme heat melts the rock into IGNEOUS ROCK

Moving plates and volcanic eruptions cause layers of rock to lift

Try Your Skills

Use the diagram below to try and work out the answers to the questions.

1. What type of rock does the sediment turn into?

2. What changes the sedimentary rock into metamorphic rock?

3. What changes rock into igneous rock?

The three types of rock are very different. Sedimentary rocks are formed when sand, shells, and pebbles gradually harden into rock. The rock is fairly soft and can contain fossils. Metamorphic rocks are formed by heat and pressure. They often have ribbonlike layers and shiny crystals. Igneous rocks are formed when melted rock cools and hardens. Sometimes it erupts from volcanoes and is called lava. When lava cools quickly it looks shiny and glasslike. Sometimes gas bubbles are trapped in the rock leaving tiny holes.

Can you guess which type of rock each of the three below are?

a)   b)   c)

Make Your Own Fossil

You will need:
- a toy dinosaur
- 4 Tbsp of dried instant coffee
- 3/4 cup of cold water
- 1 cup flour
- 6 Tbsp of salt
- a baking tray and baking paper

- Mix the instant coffee, flour, salt, and water together to make a dough.
- Put the dough on the baking tray lined with baking paper and flatten it with your palm.
- Press the dinosaur gently into the dough to make an imprint. Then remove the dinosaur.
- Bake the dough at 300°F (150°C) for 3-4 hours. Remove from the oven and leave to cool.

Head For the Hills!

Dinosaur fossil hunters have another type of map that they find useful. **Topographical** maps show the land in detail. They show all the man-made and natural features of an area. They usually show the height of the terrain using **contour** lines. Contour lines link areas that are the same height.

Relief maps are useful for finding new fossil-hunting sites. They can be used for planning a hunt, and to note the location of any dinosaur finds. Relief maps can be very useful for finding areas where fossil rocks may be found on the surface. Mines, quarries, and streams can all expose rock that would usually be buried. Fossil hunters will look for features such as these when planning a trip.

Do You Know?

About 1,500 dinosaur fossils can be seen in the rock at the Dinosaur Quarry exhibit at Dinosaur National Monument, on the Colorado and Utah border.

▲ An aerial view of the quarry at Dinosaur National Monument.

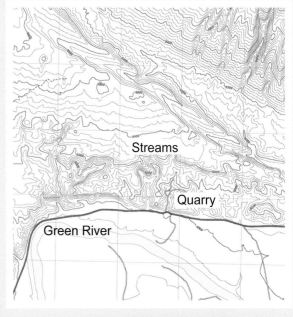

Streams

Quarry

Green River

▲ A topographical map of the same area showing the height of the mountains, the streams, and the quarry.

Help the Pteradactyls Find Dinosaur Island

If contour lines are close together, the slope is steep. If they are far apart, the slope is shallow. Can you tell which of these islands is which from their contour maps? They are not drawn to scale.

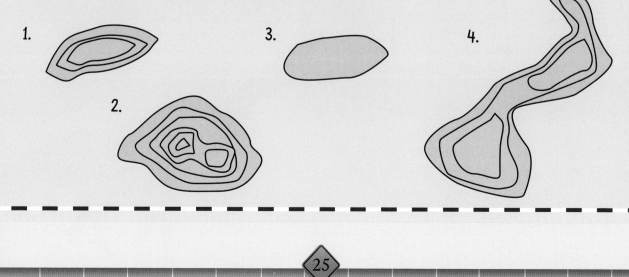

1.

3.

4.

2.

Longitude and Latitude

How do fossil hunters tell people exactly where they have found dinosaur remains? Like grid lines, lines of **longitude** and **latitude** help people find places on maps. Lines of longitude go from the top to the bottom of a globe. Lines of latitude go across the globe. The lines are numbered, so every place on the globe has its own special number. The position on the lines of latitude is always written first, followed by the position on the lines of longitude. A way to remember that is by saying "first, go up or down the rungs of a ladder-tude!"

The **prime meridian** is 0° longitude. Any lines of longitude heading west from the prime meridian are written with a W after them. Any lines of longitude heading east have an E after them. The **equator** is 0° latitude. Lines of latitude north or south of the equator have an N or an S after them.

Do You Know?

Lines of latitude are sometimes called parallels. Parallel means things are always the same distance apart.

The prime meridian is 0° longitude and passes through Greenwich in England.

Fossils of this ampelosaurus below were found in France. The location was around 45°N latitude and 0° longitude.

The equator is 0° latitude.

East or West? North or South?

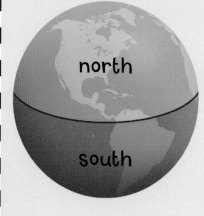

north

south

The equator separates the Earth into two **hemispheres**. The northern hemisphere is above the equator and the southern hemisphere is below. The prime meridian separates the Earth into the western and eastern hemispheres.

west   east

Look at the dinosaur map below. Which hemisphere was each dinosaur fossil found in?

1. Which dinosaurs were found in the northern hemisphere?

2. Which dinosaurs were found in the eastern hemisphere?

3. Which dinosaur was in both?

Albertaceratops   Amargasaurus   Europasaurus

Cryolophosaurus   Coelophysis   Suchomimus

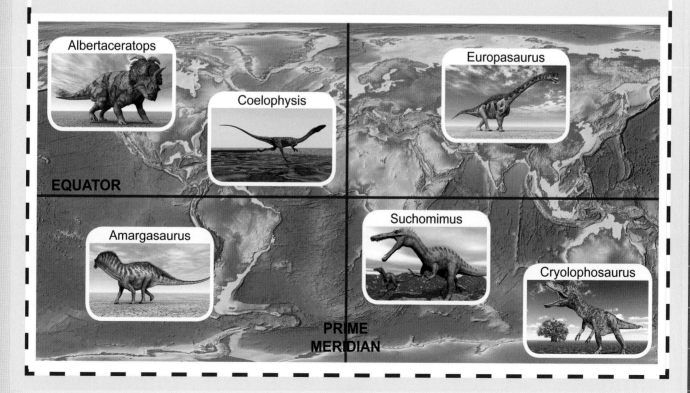

Albertaceratops

Coelophysis

Europasaurus

EQUATOR

Amargasaurus

Suchomimus

Cryolophosaurus

PRIME MERIDIAN

Why Are Dinosaurs Extinct?

Dinosaurs became extinct about 65 million years ago at the end of the Cretaceous period. The reason for this still puzzles paleontologists. Around seventy percent of animal life died out! Some animals such as frogs, fish, birds, crocodiles, and some mammals survived. Here are some of the theories.

Asteroids

Several enormous **asteroids** hit the earth around 65 million years. The impacts would have caused damage to the area, and created giant dust clouds. The dust clouds would have affected the weather. Plants would not have been able to grow, so plant-eating dinosaurs would have starved. The meat-eating dinosaurs would also have starved as they ate the plant-eaters!

Volcanoes

There was a lot of active volcanoes between 63 and 67 million years ago. The ash clouds would have had a similar effect as the asteroid cloud.

Disease

A disease may have spread and killed the dinosaurs.

Mammals

Small mammals started to compete with dinosaurs, perhaps by eating dinosaur eggs.

Paleontologists have discovered that several craters were formed at around the same time as dinosaurs became extinct. The Shiva crater in India is around 373 miles (600 km) long and 248 miles (400 km) wide! It may have been a **comet**, rather than an asteroid, that created that crater. It hit around 66 million years ago.

The 112-mile (180 km) Chicxulub crater in Mexico was created by an asteroid roughly 66 million years ago, too. The object which struck the Earth is believed to have been 6 miles (9.6 km) across!

The Boltysh crater in Ukraine is much smaller than Chicxulub. The crater is 15 miles (24 km) across. This asteroid landed on Earth a few thousand years before the Chicxulub impact.

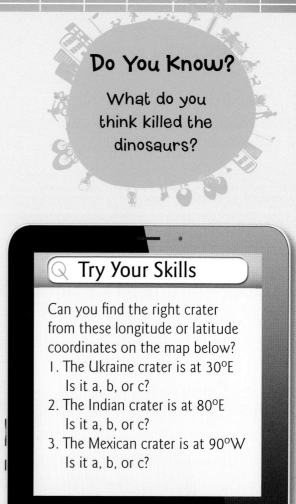

Do You Know?

What do you think killed the dinosaurs?

Q Try Your Skills

Can you find the right crater from these longitude or latitude coordinates on the map below?
1. The Ukraine crater is at 30°E
   Is it a, b, or c?
2. The Indian crater is at 80°E
   Is it a, b, or c?
3. The Mexican crater is at 90°W
   Is it a, b, or c?

A Map of Asteroid Strikes

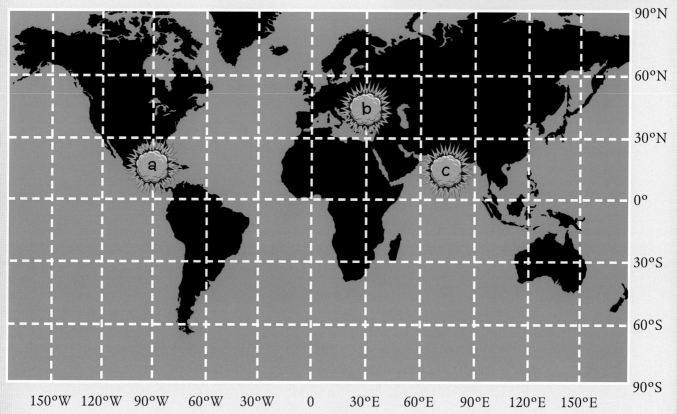

Glossary

asteroids (AS-teh-roydz)
Small bodies made of rock and iron that travel around the Sun.

axis (AK-sus)
A number line (as an x-axis or a y-axis) along which coordinates are measured.

cardinal directions
(KAHRD-nul dih-REK-shunz)
One of the four principal points of the compass: north, south, east, west.

comet (KAH-mit)
A heavenly body that has a cloudy tail as it moves closer to the sun in its orbit.

compass rose (KUM-pus ROHZ)
A drawing on a map showing directions.

continent (KON-tuh-nent)
Division of land on the globe such as North America, South America, Europe, Asia, Africa, Australia, and Antartica.

contour (KON-toor)
A line on a map connecting points with the same elevation on a land surface.

deltas (DEL-tuhs)
Areas of land made by deposits of mud and sand at the mouth of a river.

equator (ih-KWAY-tur)
An imaginary circle around the Earth equally distant from the north and south pole.

extinct (ik-STINGKT)
No longer existing.

floodplains (FLUD-playnz)
Low flat land along a stream or river that may flood.

fossils (FO-sulz)
A trace or print or the remains of a plant or animal of a past age preserved in earth or rock.

geologic (jee-uh-LAH-jik)
Relating to the rocks that make up the Earth.

grid reference (GRID REH-frens)
A point on a map defined by two sets of numbers or letters.

hemispheres (HEH-muh-sfeerz)
The halves of the Earth as divided by the equator or by a meridian.

intermediate direction
(in-ter-MEE-dee-et dih-REK-shun)
Northeast, northwest, southeast, or southwest.

latitude (LA-tih-tood)
Distance north or south from the equator, measured in degrees.

longitude (LON-jih-tood)
Distance, measured by degrees or time, east or west from the prime meridian.

north magnetic pole
(NORTH mag-NEH-tik POHL)
The direction of the Earth's
magnetic pole.

prehistoric (pree-his-TOR-ik)
Existing in times before
written history.

prime meridian
(PRYM meh-RIH-dee-en)
The meridian of 0° longitude.

projections (pruh-JEK-shunz)
A method of showing a curved surface
on a flat one.

ratio (RAY-shoh)
The relationship in quantity, amount,
or size between things.

scale (SKAYL)
Size in comparison.

sediment (SEH-deh-ment)
Material such as stones and sand
deposited by the weather.

topographical
(tah-puh-GRA-fih-kul)
Showing the heights and depths of
the features of a place.

Read More

Cooke, Tim. *Maps and Measurement*. New York: Gareth Stevens, 2010.

Coupe, Robert. *Dinosaur Hunters*. New York: PowerKids Press, 2014.

Spilsbury, Richard and Louise Spilsbury. *Fossils*. Mankato, MN: Capstone
Press, 2011.

Due to the changing nature of Internet links, PowerKids Press
has developed an online list of websites related to the subject
of this book. This site is updated regularly. Please use this link to
access the list:

www.powerkidslinks.com/fwms/dino/

Index

Answers

page 6
1 d, 2. e, 3. c, 4. b, 5. a

page 7
1. b, 2. c, 3. a
Path b crosses the lake.

page 11
d) in the cliffs

page 12
2. tree b

page 13
1. Coelophysis
2. Edmontosaurus

page 14
1. 100 times bigger,

2. 1:100, 3. 1.8 meters

page 15
1. Brachiosaurus,
2. Achelousaurus,
3. Dicraeosaurus

page 16
1. east, 2. south, 3. north,
4. west

page 17
1. east, 2. south, 3. south,
4. west

page 18
1. northeast, 2. northwest
3. southeast, 4. southwest

page 19
1. desert, 2. oceans,
3 woodland, 4. grassland

page 21
1. green, 2. there were no
dinosaurs then

page 22
1. sedimentary rock, 2. heat
and pressure, 3. heat

page 23
a) igneous, b) sedimentary,
c) metamorphic

page 25
1. Palm Island, 2. Dinosaur
Island, 3. Flat Island,
4. Long Island

page 27
1. Albertaceratops,
coelophysis, europasaurus
2. Europasaurus,
suchomimus,
crylophosaurus
3. Europasaurus

page 29
1. b, 2. c, 3. a